The Way
Everyone Is Inside

The Way
Everyone Is Inside

James Clarke

TORONTO

Exile Editions
2000

This edition is published by Exile Editions Limited,
20 Dale Avenue, Toronto, Ontario, Canada   M4W 1K4

Sales Distribution:
McArthur & Company
c/o Harper Collins
1995 Markham Road
Toronto, ON
M1B 5M8
toll free:
1 800 387 0117
(fax) 1 800 668 5788

Design and Composition by TIM HANNA
Typeset at MOONS OF JUPITER, INC. (Toronto)
Cover Painting by ADELE CLARKE
Cover Design by MICHAEL P. CALLAGHAN
Printed and Bound by MARC VEILLEUX IMPRIMEUR
Author's Photograph by JOHN REEVES

Woodcut Images are from the book
ALCHEMY by Johannes Fabricius

The publisher wishes to acknowledge
the assistance toward publication of
the Canada Council and the Ontario Arts Council.

The Canada Council
Conseil des Arts du Canada

ONTARIO ARTS
COUNCIL

CONSEIL DES ARTS
DE L'ONTARIO

ISBN 1-55096-507-7

CONTENTS

PART ONE

Rite of Passage

Legacies

From my Irish father the soft
underbelly of sentiment,

my thirsty heart.

From my French-Canadian mother
my long unbroken memory.

From my divided country the soil
to grow in.

From my dead wife the clumsy hands
that couldn't save,
the thornbush of regret.

To my children the pity.

(after R.S. Thomas)

Seven Years Old

Snow fell all night.
The Snowman filled the fire hall
yard with hills of white.

Next morning I tunnelled through
       my palace,
frolicked in its fleecy caves

       till
my sister Babe came by and
I persuaded her to dive headlong
from the firehall roof,

       watched
her nearly drown below, red
knit leggings waving in the air,
buried to the waist in snow.

The Green Hudson

Pat's mom would place forefinger to lips,
tell us to be quiet. "Your dad needs his sleep,"

she'd say. Pat's dad lived in a cloud of worry and
we quickly learned to stay out of his way.

Sunday mornings Pat's mom would load up
a wooden tray with *Detroit Times*,

LIFE, toast, jam, coffee, and tiptoe upstairs.
At noon when Pat's dad would saunter

outside we'd watch from the bushes in the
orchard as he circled his new green Hudson,

stroked its waxed curves, stood back and
admired its bright skin, amazed at the

shifting weather round his head, his worries
tumbling like ripe plums from a blue heaven.

The Gambler

(for Marilyn)

He'd park the black Cadillac in front
of the rooming house across the street,

stand on the sidewalk next to the grassy
boulevard, black shoes gleaming,

all spiffed up in homburg & dove-grey
suit, crook his baby finger to summons

my two sisters & me; then while we
watched bug-eyed he'd reach into

the grass, pronounce "abracadabra" &
presto! nickels, dimes, quarters would

flash between his diamonded fingers.
Mom told us never to take his money,

that he was a gambler who
drank too much,

didn't pay his debts. "Don't judge
a book by its cover," she'd say.

The evening the landlady found him
beside the bed already three days

dead, his gaming heart at last played
out, we lingered outside the tenement

as they brought him down the stair-
case humped on a gurney under an

old grey army blanket, polished shoes
protruding, & for the longest while

after the hearse had vanished into the
dusky air we stood there

mute, stunned dumb by the stony
face of death, the abracadabras

still ringing in our ears.

Rite of Passage

He slammed his stone fist
into my chest

sent me reeling against
the wall, gasping for air:

"Stand up and fight like a man."

I grabbed his arms, tried
to hold him close,

stop his wild thrashing;
we crashed down

the hallway like two trains
coupling

all the way to the open bed-
room door, fell

onto the bed, mute and breathless,
breastbones pressed

together, hearts beating
in unison, and

for a brief, still moment
we lay

face to face, locked
in our savage embrace,

eyes meeting,
as close as we'd ever get.

Oranges

On King Billy Day dad would
set three oranges for my two sisters

& me on the kitchen oilcloth. O
how they blazoned—big, loud, brash,

spoiling to swagger past the Fenian
church up the street, drums

beating, banners blazing, fifes
shrilling—shrunken pumpkins

in our eyes, too stiff & scary
for our tiny teeth, full

of dead men's bones.

Bullfrogs

Armed with our Daisies
and boxes of ammo
we'd hike to Calley's Creek,
sneak up on the enemy
sunning themselves on the smooth wet rocks.

How we thrilled
as they leapt high in the air and flopped
                                on their backs
in the coppery creek,
goggled-eyed and still,
                                a pellet lodged
within the brain
or bulging like a piece of shiny shrapnel
from a creamy chest.

We never ate their sleek, fat legs,
our only hunger was to kill, kill.

Wartime Mommy

As the sun began to set
my two sisters would shout

"Mom's back"
& we'd rush to meet her

as she rounded the firehall,
her flats

clacking on the bright orange
bricks, white uniform

aureoled in golden light, three
melting ice cream cones

balanced in her
fist.

Evening when I
was supposed

to be asleep, I'd spy on her
through the old stovepipe

hole in bedroom
floor, as she sat alone near

the kitchen door, a naked
light bulb above her head,

swollen feet in a green basin,
face white, the weight

of loneliness slipping from her.

Prophecy

(for Dick)

1949 was the year I almost drove
mom crazy. At school I spent my hours

staring out the window, woolgathering.
The nuns told me I was wasting my

time, committing a mortal sin. "God
counts on us to do our best," they said.

My school was Spiro's Poolroom, learning
to be 'shark' just like Ace Howard,

who'd boxed professionally & once quipped
after whistling the blue smoke from

his cue, slick as a gunslinger, that he
was in Baghdad when I was still in my

dad's bag. I kept a pack of Sweet Caps
in my hip pocket, raided dad's booze

whenever I got the chance (I had to be
sly, he kept a close eye) & hung out

with Frenchy Lavasseur, a pimply-
faced six footer, two years my senior,

who'd tool me around town in his green
Ford jalopy to ogle the chicks.

O how worldly & sexy we felt! Frenchy's
dad was a giant with pink cheekbones who

always reeked of whisky; every fall after
the hunt he'd hang his trophies outside

his butcher shop for all the town to gawk at;
that November he shot a bear, lashed a wire

around his neck & hooked it to a wooden
gallows, glazed eyes bulging, pink tongue

hanging out, cool autumn gusts ruffling its
black hairs. I shuddered when I touched

its cold, curled claws & glimpsed Frenchy's
old man in his bloodied apron, thick square

shoes planted firmly on the sawdust floor
behind the meat block, cleaver in fist.

Frenchy & I left school that year at Christmas—
he to work in the shop, me to wash

dishes at the Old Empress for 20 cents an hour—
my first taste of the real world, mom said

fulfilling her prophecy that I'd end up a nobody
just like dad.

Local Hero

Every Sunday I visit him
in the centre of the town park,
his larger-than-life effigy almost olympian
atop the marble monument
decked out in bronze battledress,

                                  rifle at the ready,
jaw tilted toward sky, resolute
look in eye—the long descending list of dead
                                      unscrolling beneath his feet.

We don't talk much (he was never one for words), but
occasionally he'll bark:
"Don't slouch lad, walk like a man," and I'll have to
tuck in chin, square shoulders, look smart.
                                    Lately, I've noticed
his pallor has turned a sickly
green.
I have to admire his quiet doggedness.

He never lacks for company. A small band of
pigeons love to preen themselves
                                    on his shoulders,
land on his helmet, burble in his ear.
But even when they streak
                              his shiny face
with daubs of white—how embarrassing to have
to wipe his nose—
he never flinches or complains.

And in the evening when I have to leave,
dewy-eyed at parting as I always am,
he'll stiffen his upper lip and snap:
"Soldiers never cry lad."
—his blind, unblinking eyes darkening in the dusk.

Ceremonies of the Hearth

The lore of hardwood groves, the rites
of firewood stir my blood; split

logs (sawn into handy chunks) speak
of forethought as my aged father used

to say; he taught me to appreciate the
sturdy chopping block, the sharply bevelled

blade, the zen of the swift, severing blow;
You can buy wood sawn, split and dried

I know (I've bought a cord or two
I'm ashamed to say), but it's not

the same. So when father asks:
"Has Jim got his wood in yet?"

I have to turn away. Jim left home years
ago, hopped a ride in a Ryder truck, lit

out for parts unknown and we haven't seen
him since.

Father might just as well have asked:
"Does Jim take tea?" for he hated wood

cleaving, the small ceremonies of the hearth.
Now the season of memory's here

you'll probably find him somewhere
adrift in yellow leaves, listening

to the fluting of the wind or burnishing
a poem. But snow's in the air and I

know my father's mind; he won't give up.
"Has Jim got his wood in yet?" he'll say again.

Home

Not anymore the steep edge
of the field, the wet sedge,

not anymore the pins of light in
polar night;

I have fitted my hand to the latch,
the sloping roof, found

that haven in the mind where
kisses, bread, talk

are cradled, the gravity of the
world lifted,

a place to hold onto against
the long hours of emptiness,

the irremediable cold.

Undercoat

(for Paul)

My son, the teacher, who's helping me paint
the four Victorian-style screen doors I

bought for the cottage, knows my habits better
than myself, spreads papers on the deck where

I'll be working, tells me to leave spindles, ginger-
bread, the wood around the knobs for him.

"And don't load up your brush," he says. "Remember,
less is more." We divide the paint (premium quality

primer—"the best always lasts"), & go about our separate
tasks but, not before he chides me to slow down.

"Life's too short," he says. I watch him kneeling by
the bunky door below, Bach's *Magnificat*

on the radio; he doesn't slap on paint like me; his
strokes are soft & sure, caress the wood; occasionally

he stops, inspects his work, retouches—the epitome
of mindfulness. "Painting's a form of meditation,"

he loves to say. Afterwards he looks at my flecked
face & skin, shows me his clean hands & grins.

What Are You Staring At?

(for Clair)

Around November 1947
> Sister Mary crooks her baby finger
> to summons me to the front of the class,
> tells me I'd better
> start looking for a job in a
> factory. "You've got as much chance of
> graduating as a chicken passing through
> that keyhole," she announces, pointing
> to the door. That Christmas Mike & I
> drop out, get jobs as busboys at the
> Empress.

Around December 1933:
> A few days before Christmas, mom
> brings me home in a taxi from the hospital.
> Dad & Mick Collins
> are in the kitchen, three sheets to the
> wind, an empty wine jug on the table
> between them. When mom asks where the gifts
> are, dad says: "I gave you a boy, isn't that
> good enough?"

Around August 1948:
> I try to kiss Sylvia Sullivan, my
> school crush, in the back seat of Bugsy's
> dad's Hudson, but miss her mouth,
> graze the chin instead. Sylvia
> shoots me one of her grand piano smiles.
> I spot flecks of spinach between her
> perfect teeth. "What are you staring
> at?" she says.

Around September 1946:
>   I listen on the upstairs landing
>   to the McCoys at the front door
>   telling mom they will no longer want their son to
>   associate with me. "Bobby's going places
>   even if your son isn't."

Around April 1948:
>   When I tell Mike at the Silver Moon
>   that I've made up my mind to go back to school,
>   he laughs out loud, says I'll only be
>   spinning my tires.

Around July 1944:
>   Canon Robertson from St. John's
>   visits us. My two sisters & me are sent
>   outside to play while he talks to mom
>   in the parlour alone. Afterwards, I hear
>   from the bedroom her stifled sobs. Gaby tells
>   us to hush, that dad's been shot in Normandy.
>   "But don't worry," she says, "he'll live."

Around May 1952:
>   I give a speech before the student
>   body at the high school about the importance
>   of the Security Council at the U.N.,
>   going public for the first time with my new David
>   Niven accent. I notice my friends wince, hunker
>   in their seats. Later
>   Sister Lucretia calls me
>   to the office.
>   "I never knew you'd lived in England,
>   Jim," she says.

Around October 1945:

   We go to the CPR train station for
   Dad's homecoming. A stranger in khaki
   greatcoat with golden buttons lifts me high
   over his head, scrapes his prickly jaws
   against my cheeks.

Around August 1951:

   Dad chases my youngest sister into
   the parlour, takes off his belt, says
   he's going to teach her a lesson.
   I grab his arm. "Touch her again & I'll
   kill you."

Around June 1947:

   Mémère, my French-Canadian grand-
   mother agrees to drape the cuffs of my
   new grey flannels for the Teen Town Dance
   —all my friends are wearing drapes—
   but doesn't understand, sews the leggings
   into stovepipes so tight I can't get into
   them.

On April 8th 1990 (Palm Sunday 2 pm to be exact):

   My wife drives the grey New Yorker
   to Niagara Falls & never comes back.

Around January 1968:

              I visit Dad at Sunnybrook where
he's gone for an operation—
carpal tunnel syndrome the doctors call
it. I watch as he spoon-feeds an old comrade
who lost both arms in Normandy; he's quiet
& courteous, eager to know about my work
the wife, our kids. He hasn't had a drink in over
a week; it's like talking to a stranger.

Around May 1997:

              I publish *Silver Mercies*, my first
book of poetry.

PART TWO

Diving Instructions
at the
Great Barrier Reef

Tasmania

Here on the shore
at Southport

the vast southern
ocean unscrolling

before me in the
dark, polar

air breathing on
my neck, the white

stars stab like
stalactites into

my dolomite heart as I
cling to the

edge of the world,
the biting lust

in me—a weightless
spark in

the cavern
of the night.

Rainy Season Queensland

In the sky's unbottled glut
              here at Karanda
the rains weep
              small tears, many
hues of blue;
              the forest floor
is cool and dark and deep.

I think of you,
              the gap
of your long absence,
              thirst again
for the bright lianas
              that bind the heart
and world together.

Like the cassowary
              I feed on fallen
fruit, spread
              seed everywhere,
new roots under the dark canopy.

On the Rim

When he observed her walking
along the path toward the limestone cliffs

on the Great Ocean Road—graveyard
of many wrecks—stop at the rim and

glance down at the surf battering its
white knuckles against the stone-ribbed

walls of the gorge 100 metres below—
the rock stacks of the Twelve Apostles

looking benignly on—the old grief
came surging back, his heart

stalled and a lump swam in his throat
as he ached to shout:

"Stop, stop, don't jump" till at last
her voice rang out, clear, sharp

as a silver bell: "Dad, Dad, it's
beautiful here," and the dark spell broke.

At the Apostle Inn

(found poem)

8 april 98

> It is my pleasure to stay here. For us it is
> first visit to Great Ocean Road and twelve
> apostles. Thank you very much for your
> arrangements. I feel like stay at home.
>
> > Wan & Shak
> > (from Malaysia)

8/5/99

> We think it was very nice and very clean.
> Good T.V. and kettle. That's all.
>
> > The Lambs
> > Rod, Ruby, Roy & Ruth

25 June 1999

> It's gonna be better if we could have
> one mirror in front of toilette. Then
> one could dress without waiting while
> someone's inside. What do you think?
>
> > Billy,
> > U.S.A.

31 June 1999

> ho, ho, ho, ha, ha, ha, huh, huh, huh
> I love this place baby! It's really cool.
>
> > S.

14 Sept 99

       Nice & quiet, spacious, spotlessly
       clean, but needs more hooks in the
       bathroom. Can you tell me what it
       is with the picture of the picnic at
       Boggy Creek (eek! who'd want to
       buy such a thing.) And how about some
       new couches, maybe pink to go with
       the curtains & a dishwasher; we came
       here on holiday, not to wash dishes,

                        remember?
       Do you live here? My name is Friz.
       I'm six years old

                      Friz

14/12/99

       Very clean, comfortable, like home away
       from home. Thanks.

                      Andre.

10?/1/200

       So far we've tied up the donkey &
       took off the saddle bags. The pesky
       moths are invading their sun—our
       bloody ceiling light. Drove the G.O.R.
       last night with my eyes shut. The twelve
       apostles showed me the light. Nice big
       bed—ah! we put it to good use.

                  Ruth & Michael
                    (Canada)

15 Jan 2000

Very good stay. Very clean. australians
lovely peoples.

Vincenzio & Maria

(Italia)

28.1.2000

We thought the place was very nice but
the sickening niceties of the previous occupants
in the guest book, filling the slightly boring
wait before they left, make me want to puke.
How many pints had the fellow harping about
the donkey, drank?
What was the critic of the bathroom hooks
thinking?
Will the mirror on the bathroom wall be
o.k. for that person when he/she returns?
Will he/she ever return?
And who cares.   Francis & Ann

(Ireland)

P.S. Thanks for everything.

Prayer for Travellers

Father, look kindly on those doomed to travel the earth,
taking photographs, mailing post cards, buying made-in-

Taiwan souvenirs, & walking around in drip-dry nylon
underwear. Give them wisdom in the selection of

hotels, that they may find their reservations honoured &
hot water running in the taps. We pray that the telephone

works, the operator speaks English & that e-mail is
available. Lead them to inexpensive restaurants where

the food is superb, the waiter friendly & the wine
complimentary. Light their paths with sunshine & photo-

opportunities & spare them the affliction of dogs, horses,
& fellow-travelling bores. Forgive, too, their inability

to tip. Make the locals love them for who they are,
not what they can do for the economy. Grant them

the stamina to visit museums, cathedrals, national
parks, colonial houses, convict gaols, no matter

how depressing dull and dreary. And if, perchance,
they should falter & fail to see

an historic site in order to nap after lunch, have mercy
on their willing, but weak flesh. AMEN.

Diving Instructions at the Great Barrier Reef

You only get one set of fins.
Use them wisely. Fins are for swimming,
not walking, should fit snug and comfortable.
Fin gently, keep legs straight.

Everyone should have a mask. The brine
stings. Children wear small masks, adults
wear large masks. To prevent fogging
spit on the inside of the glass.

Never touch the reef. If you dive look and
reach up before you surface; there may be
somebody above you. Look up often
to check how far you've gone, you may

have strayed farther than you think. Know
your limits and abilities. Stay within the boundaries.
If you're having difficulty wave your hands
above your head. Above all, forget

your troubles. Remember, you're part of the
world's seven wonders; relax, breathe deeply
and cultivate the moment. Take only photos and
memories, leave only bubbles.

One last blast of the whistle signals the end
of the dive, the time to turn in fins and masks,
make room for the next guest.

The Reef

How odd the denizens of the reef;
cuttlefish speak an arcane tongue;

harlequins are exhibitionists, their blue teeth
glow fluorescent; sting-rays flatten

on the sand, jolt you when they shake
your hand; jellies and hydroids sting.

On the spiny coral reef love pries loose,
the luminous gives way to grief; puffer-

fish purse poison lips; the Southern
Peacock's milk will kill; life is

quirky, brief, oblique and while some
bluff or mimic those with stronger

teeth and others shift their skin and sex
at will, the majority's content to play

at hide-and-seek. Are they happy or
merely fluttery like a flock

of sheep? Who can say. How odd
the denizens of the deep.

Japanese Valises on the Road
to Fiordland Forests

At the entrance
                of the Te Anau Motor Inn
off by themselves in
                the raw first light

the luggage congregates;
                black & white valises,
same size, same make,

                huddled together
shoulder to shoulder
                in line like sheep,

waiting for
                the sun to rise
like a divine wind &
                sweep them up to
the Floating Bridge of Heaven.

Aubade

Here I am back from the troubled
dream coast, my imagination floating
on a mattress of fleece; morning slides
wafers of sunlight under my lids, bats
put away their caps & hide. Look!
the green catalpa's turned white, blue
jays are scuffling in the trees. O Sun,
open wide your silken wings, let me
linger in this room of light, that separate
place between thought & felt, my mind
swept clean by the broom of peace.

Gardening Hints

Fall weather's unpredictable, the gardener says,
you have to learn to live with frost; a sharp

chill will kill your proud roses, your lush tomatoes,
your delicate beans, churn your green

garden into a stiff sea of clods. You can put up
a good fight, build lean-to's (old storm windows will

do), pile on thick blankets of mulch, put cardboard,
towels, old brooms, newspaper, plastic to

cunning use, even bring fruit and veggies indoors to
ripen on sills in pleasant sun-bright rooms,

but in the end nothing holds; the light
will fail and the hardiest of the lot—cauliflower,

apples, turnips, leeks—shall fall; there's no way
                    to stop the cold; in the land

God gave Cain, ice conquers all.

Flux

Under the melting snow
a red tricycle takes shape,

apple blossoms, lighter
than the blue silk sky,

stream before my eyes;
seasons come & go,

but no matter how gently
I touch the rose the petals

will fall, the soft circle
round the fire will break &

leaf by leaf the darkening
trees grow cold;

the long goodbyes never
seem to cease, nothing

stays the same or whole.

PART THREE

Lottery of Justice

Retaining Wall

(for Norm)

My neighbour at the lake is worried about his retaining
wall. "The cedar logs are buckled & decayed," he

says, "we should have stripped the bark, but didn't."
He's made a crib of railway ties, cobbled together

with 12 " spikes, rigged a V-shaped chute lined with
roof metal & ordered 100 yards of sand. "You're too

old for this," I say, grab a long-handled spade, load up
barrow & shovel sand down the chute—mucky

work which makes the muscles ache. "There's got to be
an easier way to make a buck." Occasionally

we take a break, lean on shovels to catch our breath
& ruminate, mostly about our losses: his first wife's

cancer, "at the end she was only skin & bones,"
his only daughter's death on the 401, my wife's

suicide. "There are holes you can never fill," he says. We
put in two-hours shifts, twenty loads an hour—about 200

shovelfuls of sand—trekking back & forth between sandpile &
chute. The hill of sand never seems to fade, the crib's a

bottomless pit; "We just have to keep going," he says.
"I want to build a wall that stays."

The Gate

(for R.G. Thomas)

After he delivered a judgment (and before
his next case) the judge
liked to retreat to his chambers, cover
his eyes
        with a black, silk mask &
take a nap.

He'd see a gate
        open, golden, wide,
a guardian angel graven on its side,
a scene so bright,
        it filled his dream with light,
but when he woke the gate
        was always gone

as though a sleeve had smudged the slate
        leaving him,
brightness dimmed,
frailties intact
        to walk alone
the long dark hall of justice.

Five Easy Pieces

I

Divorce proceedings:
the leaves unhook
& fly.

II

Bitter recriminations:
I envy the dog
who wags his tail.

III

Pileated lawyers
pecking at the bark of law,
looking for openings.

IV

In the corridor a stray
cat licks its paws &
yawns.

V

Day in the Halls of Justice:
nothing to remind me
the sun is shining.

Buried in Snow

(for Bob Zelinski)

How odd I know

                    to overhear oneself say

at 3 o'clock

                    on a winter's day:

"We want the truth,

                    the whole truth &

nothing but the truth,"

                    a blizzard blowing

cold blue needles

outside the courtroom window.

Tribal Customs

(for Justice Speyer)

Lawyers love to beat dead horses;
when the horse won't move they

buy stronger whips, change riders.
Sometimes the government appoints

a committee to visit race tracks,
stables, paddocks, clubhouses—

all the favourite watering holes.
Invariably the committee will

set new standards for riding and
recommend that no one dismount,

which leads to the present
craze—a phenomenon that never

ceases to amaze—lawyers proud
in the saddle like Gary Cooper,

astride several dead horses harnessed
together for greater speed,

prancing on the same spot repeatedly
and going nowhere in a great hurry.

Lottery of Justice

(Port Arthur penal colony
    Van Diemen's land.)

Francis Curtis, of Exeter, stealing a pair of shoes,   seven years.
James Coyne, of Leeds, stealing a canister of tea,   seven years.
Thomas Challin, of Kent, stealing two looking glasses,   life.
Joseph Crapp, of Devon, stealing a loaf of bread,   fourteen years.

John Frederick, of Devon stealing a Bible,   fourteen years.
Richard Dunn, of Cornwall, stealing a bundle of candles,   seven years.
Robert Davies, of Sussex, stealing a pocket handkerchief,   life.
Charles Chapman, of Essex, stealing a turkey,   fourteen years.

William Yeoman, of Shropshire, pickpocketing,   seven years.
Felix Daley, of Liverpool, stealing silver spoons,   fourteen years.
James Boxhall, of Sussex, pickpocketing a gentleman,   life.
William Lacey Cooper, of the Old Bailey, stealing a flute,   life.

A Sad Tale

The old judge woke one morning
        bedsheets rumpled,
                chest cracked open like a husk,
                    gasping for air.

Instantly he knew the thing
        he dreaded most—the occupational
                hazard his colleagues talked about
                had happened:

his heart had flown, sprung from its rib cage
        without a trace
                in the dead of night while he
                lay dreaming

of the wheel of perfect justice.
        A note dangling from the bedroom door:
                After years of neglect, the heart said,
                I can't take it any more.

In the War Zone

of Family Court everyone
                    is always racing somewhere;
spouses race to make war,
                    judge & lawyers race
to make words,
                    write dispatches, &
children race to make trenches,
                    cover their faces,
listen to the distant artillery fire.

A Bump the Size of a Dime

Until his accident, the plaintiff
led a normal life. The damage was so minor—
dent in trunk—the police were not called. The
doctor who examined his injuries—a bump on the forehead
the size of a dime—prescribed Tylenol lll, told him to get some
rest.

But he got migraines, couldn't eat, couldn't
sleep. X-rays, CAT-scans, MRI's, proved
negative. He quit driving, stopped bowling,
missed work. He found he could no longer make
love to his wife. The psychiatrist diagnosed
anxiety; he tried acupuncture, massages,
home exercises but nothing worked. Eventually
he lost his job, spent most of his day holed up in the basement
watching game shows. When his wife couldn't take it any
longer, she packed her
bags, grabbed the kids, and moved out.

Last week his lawyer came to court seeking a million dollars.
"My client was born with a thin skull," he said.

Vigilante Justice

She lived with a group of six women,
she said, all student nurses like herself.
One told them how she had been sexually
assaulted in the parking lot of the nursing
residence. Somehow they suspected the
perpetrator would return to the scene &
when he showed up a week later, they
were ready.

"Before he knew what was happening
we'd surrounded his car," she said.
"I still remember his small, dark
moustache, the way his upper lip
trembled. He tried to run but we had
baseball bats & crowbars & he never
had a chance. We swarmed all over him.
Sometimes at night I still shudder at
how savage we were, how little
mercy we showed. When we were
done we left him on the pavement, naked
& unconscious, but still alive."

She paused, took a sip of wine.
"I can't tell you what happened to him
after that," she said. "I only know he'll
never rape again."

Humiliation of the Word

Frazzled by the barrage of images from
the Cyclop's eye—that sensual wraparound

world that holds us all in thrall—and
worried about the escalating humiliation

of the Word, I repair to that haven
of the linear page, the local

library, where surrounded by stacks of
books I hope

to catch again (if only for a time)
the genie of Print,

the dispassionate, hoarded powers
of the mind, only

to find not the detachment I so sorely
craved but an oaken table

graven with valentines, cupids, lips,
penises and other

libidinous runes: "Hello, I want to
shag," "Fern gives good head," "Kelly's

hot stuff," "Brad's a fag," "Eat
me on the table," etc. etc.

Even in paradise turns the crooked worm.

Canadian Lovers

A pot
                of P.E.I. spuds,

jackets missing,
                eyes gouged,

roots amputated,
                beaten into

a multi-cultural pulp &
                smothered in thick

Charter sauce,
                a picnic for two,

bland as spring clouds
                totally indigestible to strangers.

The Achy-Breaky Foot

In this country, a nation of foot-
sloggers, we talk about feet.

At night we sit before
the wood stove
feet up,

                & complain
our corns are killing us,
footpads are wearing thin,
our spine is misaligned;
we say the government don't care,
that the shoe don't fit.

Oh supinating foot!
Oh pronating foot!

The separatist *se plaint*,
threatens to walk barefoot
in the snow,

                bunioned & alone.

Oh loneliness of the achy-breaky foot!

Old loyalists and oil patch reformers
know the problem: *planter fasciitis:*
inflammation

                          of the connective tissue,
insist all should buy their
hand-tooled boot   where
every foot, A to triple A,
has room to breathe.

Oh desolation of the deformed foot!
Oh poetry missing a foot!
Oh the athlete's foot!
The constitutional sore foot!

Oh Dr. Scholl of the silk-lined insole,
make us whole again!

Pass the Butter

Pass the butter, pappy, oops,
did I say butter? I mean pass
the margarine o.k. & don't forget
to pass the ut. mi. & re. – you see,
I love the crazy quilt of words in
the morning.

And I like ketchup with my ut., salt
with my mi., & coffee with my re.; so
while you're at it, pass the ketchup,
salt, & coffee along with the ut. mi.
& re. &

remember to add a pinch of pepper, o.k. &
make it snappy, pappy, my hunger is Homeric,
no, that's too exalted, I mean I'm hungrier
than a nuthatch & I love the crazy quilt
of words in the morning.

Please Write Soon

I love letters spun from the transparent
fibres of the heart: nothing stimulates

me more than the flutter of mail pushing
through the slot like moths. I

keep them close at hand, the way a flamenco
dancer holds a fan, change continents

just to fondle their delicate frames. Today
alas, bills, notices, circulars by the

score, but letters scarcely any more,
faded like ghostly silhouettes on

a darkened screen; even letters to get
letters are of no avail; intimacy travels

so swiftly these days my news is always
stale; friends tell me when I complain

that I must get e-mail. O for the bloom
of handwriting on a page—the porous

human smudge! A perfect printout is never
quite the same. Please write soon.

Blind River

Seven a.m. & here I am
stretched on a lawn chair
                down by the lake
gazing at the red & blue fishing boats
along the shore,

                a coke can
bobbing in the bay, when
the American tourist
                biting on a bad cigar,
a bald eagle: DON'T RUFFLE MY FEATHERS
emblazoned on his white muscle t-shirt
                spots me &
hustles over to give me the big "five"
& before I can put down my poetry (Bruce Wiegl's
Archeology of the Circle)
I'm wrapped in plumes of smoke and words
                gasping for air,
how they kicked ass in Kosovo and showed Milosevic
you can't fool with Uncle Sam blah, blah,
why race problems in his country have been exaggerated
& how back home in Evansville, Indiana
he works with five "nigras"
& no problem as long as they do their job blah, blah, blah,
& what the Cuban crisis really needs
is a Republican President to sit down with Fidel
for a couple of hours
to tell him the facts of life blah, blah, blah, blah...

& then maybe, he says
we could get some of them real good Havanas to suck on.

The Scary Thing

is you can say anything:

that the diamond solitaire just below the place
you love to be kissed will slow your breathing;

that all you need for happiness is an island where
the pulse slows in time to the undulating waves &
you can hear the song of the kisadee miles away;

that those shiny appliances will take the frazzle
out of your marriage;

that the revolutionary skin serum with 8% Mexican yam will
soothe the torrential inner sanctum of your body & give you peace;

that this new seductive perfume will make you drop your
broom & raise hell;

that the line between sensuality & safety no longer
exists in your automobile;

that your garden will be the talk of the beehive,

and someone will believe you.

Garlic Jar

(for Mary Rutherford)

I lift it
to the light,
jade-coloured, ringed like Saturn,
ash deposits
on its fire face, a circlet
of eight air holes
near the base.

The potter's note says
it was ripened
in a river of fire—a two-
chambered "Japanese Style"
climbing kiln—wood-stoked
for twenty hours.

So simple!
I wish I had its secret!
   No showing off,
just a plain vessel
   glazed with love.

PART FOUR

The Way
Everyone Is Inside

Lonely Couple

Pegged together on the clothesline

                   in the backyard

a pair of faded jeans &

                  a yellow cotton dress

shiver side by side—

                        dreaming of fire,

the intimacy of the bedroom—

                        twisting in the bone-

chilling wind, season after

                        season, no one

to take them in.

The Itch

Last night I had the strongest itch
to hold you in my arms and kiss you,

but wisely I refrained, knowing
that if I hadn't I might have caused

an epidemic, the incurable itch
passing from lip to lip,

until the world became one big,
itching mouth. Imagine the blow

to the economy if everyone took time
to scratch the itch to love.

Epithalamium

(for Mira and Bruce)

Grown beyond yourselves
        you decide
to share one life, housed
        in one another's arms,
even unto death. Love
        has made you brave.

We, the witnesses,
        mindful of our defections,
long to cry out:
        The journey is too hard,
but deep within us,
        some grace
stirred by fresh beginnings
        sweeps aside our cowardice,
brims our hearts to sweet excess,
        till at last
we dare to sing:
        "Yes O Yes."

Manual to Jump-Start Yout Wedding
(found poem)

Set off a sure-fire signal that the fun
starts the moment you've pronounced

your vows by dancing down the aisle
to a cozy salsa, a rousing "R & B" or

a rock 'n' roll tune; hire a violinist to
romance your receiving line or entertain

your guests with a mime artist, magician, or
fortune teller; and don't leave them

cooling their heels; have waiters stroll
around with munchies & drinks. Top

your wedding cake with sculpted marzipan
figures to show off your respective careers or

even distinguishing physical features; if one
of you is short, show it! If you met on

vacation have your figures in bathing suits,
carrying tennis rackets etc. A great ice-

breaker for guests is to make finding their
seats a game; identify each table with

a wildflower or the title of a movie; guests
will enjoy asking other guests if they've

seen *From Here to Eternity* or
the Lady's Slipper; keep the mood

lively by encouraging guests to bid you
to kiss (all in the spirit of fun, of course) but

make them work for it. Have them make a
hole-in-one at a mini-putt set which you can

set up at the entrance to the reception.
Finally end the festivities with a real bang.

Gather everyone in the garden for a personal
fire-works display.

Dear Thérèse

I confess I've been feeling
faint-hearted & restless lately.
Your suggestion of a health salad
sounds just fine. Among
the 5700 Chinese herbal medicines
there's one called Jujube;
I don't know much about it except
it has a sweet pleasant taste &
the Chinese have been using it
for 2500 years—a closely kept
secret—to nourish the
heart & quieten the spirit;
I'll have to go down to Chinatown though
to buy some — I'll take along the *Encyclopedia
of Medicinal Herbs* just in case—while
you pick spinach from Palma's garden &
sip Vichy water to keep your metabolism
on track. And don't worry, I'll be back;
I want a long life just like Confucius,
to be organic just like you,
                    tangled, leafy, fit;
my jejune heart needs a retrofit.

Night

I lie on the dock &
                    shut my eyes
against the rush of sun;
                    a wall of fire
burns inside my skull.

I cover lids
                    with both palms,
but still the flames
                    peep through.

I press the sockets with
                    all my might till
sun's devoured &
                    nothing's left,
not even a gasp of light.

Was it Night like this, I ask,
that made you climb the parapet
                    & leap?

Relic

The last I saw of her alive
she was in bed; she blew
a kiss, waved farewell, she'd
see me when I got back, she said.

Almost ten years to the day as I
rummaged in our dresser drawers
preparing for a holiday, a perfume
bottle—amber the colour

of her hair—poked up from under
a mound of socks & underwear,
fluted, hard, like an ancestral bone
breaking through the sod, or

a dark shell you'd find upon
a beach, ground round & smooth &
bare by the scraping of the sea, a relic
from another world, empty of all

being, the long ocean in between.

The Crossing

She waited on the dock for the ferry
to the outer isles, a man beside her—

companion or lover I couldn't say—
with long, wise mien, and as sea

roiled and licked its green tongue at
dark clouds I felt fearful

—such a rough and perilous crossing—
till I observed the tender way

he gazed at her, the radiance on
her seamless face, as though

skin, eyes, brimmed with inner light,
a hidden sun, and then I knew

she had returned to her beginnings,
the sun-warmed place of giving and

receiving, and was cherished as she'd
always deserved to be, more

than I could ever love, and all
my sadness turned to joy.

Damselfly in September

Stealthily she glides
above the cottage deck,

a black speck against
the sky, then, suddenly,

stops, hovers a half-
second and drops

down an invisible thread
to perch upon my chair,

abdomen-elongate,
jacket, metallic blue,

large eyes touching on
top of head,

four lacy wings—stone
still, a solitary

creature like me, just
passing through,

pausing for its moment
in the sun.

Winter Prayer

When we arrive the lake
is muffled in glass; overnight

earth finds a new language; pine
boughs breathe white words,

mica shavings carol in the air;
black-hooded chickadees spin &

whirl on invisible threads from
cedars to Palma's feeder, gorging

on oilseed. Rodrique says they
stay all winter, sheltering from

the cold in the angles of the limbs.
I gaze at the stars shivering

in their deep blue caves. How long
O Lord before your sun's reborn,

my frozen heart is thawed?

Beloved

I love the smell of woodsmoke,
the smooth skin of stones,
the shape of a baby's toes;
I loved

                         your clear eyes too
where I could see forever,
their gentle "yes" to all;
I won't accept
        they've fallen
              into

                    the

                          deep

                                down

                                      blue
beyond my ken.
Love is like death
              only longer.

Letter

Dear Robert Redford: I get so sad when I look back.
Is it the same for you? I know you won't remember but

we had tea together in Kitzbühel in 1968. You were
there to make *Downhill Racer*; I was an unpaid

extra, part of the jubilant crowd that rushed you after
your big win (my moment of glory, alas, a victim of

the cutting floor). My wife thought you were wonderful
—"so natural," she said, as you steered the

conversation to our work with the mentally handicapped
in France, never once talking about yourself. We had

something in common at the time: young families and careers
(you and Lola had three children); the memory of

living on bouillon in an Upper East Side walkup must have
been still fresh in your mind, but the future looked golden.

Where has the time gone? The other day I looked at
your photo in *People Magazine*— the same

youthful blond mane, big white smile, chiselled features—
& I couldn't believe it! You've hardly changed.

Is it true that you're not afraid of aging? By the way
I loved your last picture *The Horse Whisperer*;

the role of Tom Booker the Zen-like cowboy who
knew how to gentle horse & people suited you.

Of course all this happened before *Butch Cassidy
and The Sundance Kid* & your ascension into

celluloid heaven; before the breakup of your marriage
(a divorce you didn't want) and the suicide of my wife;

long before both of us were forced to jump into
the raging waters.

The Way Everyone Is Inside

What are you doing with your life?
This is a good Buddhist question.
You didn't buy it.
It's quite sobering, but the way
the world is being organized, bigger parts
of it are sliding inexorably into
smaller, where we live,
we don't even know we're being bruised.

When the raging elephant (or angry
boss, it makes no difference) comes charging
it's already too late.

The old millennium is darkening like a window,
the bus is breaking down:
ball bearings have sprung loose, we're desperately
in need of a cosmic catching mitt—a fresh way
of seeing;
a new sun's begging to be born.

Requiem for a Mosquito

Don't kill it, said the Buddhist,
showing me a close-up

of its hairy, alien face. See,
a marvel of genetic engineering,

like the Stealth that circles out of
sight, equipped with infraradiation

to spike you in the night. The biggest
bloodsucker on the Ark

is Man, he said, not this humble
creature who only sips

five-millionths of a litre. I listened
patiently to what he had to say,

then squashed the critter anyway.

Satori in Surin

The old monk led me
into the inner courtyard;
above us perched the

Buddha on his lacquered
dais—a golden pear.
Doves burbled on the

ivied walls, fragrance
of jasmine filled the air, a
breeze ruffled the skin

of the pool. The old monk
clasped my hand; the pool
rilled with tiny suns;

I thought I heard the tinkle
of bells from far away. There
was a breath of wings, a

tremble of light as though
a dark bird had flown
from my brow. Something

happened; I do not know.

Kindred Spirits

The Virgin & Buddha
would make a fine couple,
they've so much in common,
their differences are subtle.

The Virgin lives in a bathtub
of rocks; the Buddha reclines
on a dais of gold; yet
they're always the same, never
grow old &
neither wears socks.

The Virgin stays out in all kinds
of weather, but never
gets wet; her clothes are
immaculate. The Buddha

nibbles on lichee & rice,
keeps his eyes closed,
& neither is prone to arthritis
or vice.

Their heads are so groovy with
celestial thought, no one
would say they are funny;
the Virgin spends all her

time adoring her Son while
Buddha just squats
on his tummy.

I love the Virgin,
I love the Buddha,
I wish we were friends &
could go to the movies together.

The Steeple

(for Father Kevin)

I climbed to the top
        of the old stone church,
sneaked up the staircase
        to the choir loft, ascended
the ladder to the windy belfry;
        steeple swayed,
splinters scratched my face,
        nails tore my clothes
as I groped skyward
        into that narrowing space,
darkness round me closing
        like a trap,
fearful, perhaps I had gone too far,
        till at last I bumped my head
against the Cross,
        discovered I had nowhere else to turn.

Last Caravan to Damascus

(for Gay & Graham)

A singularly bleak December it was,
cold, icy, our bodies flaring in the winter
moonlight; we cut a deal with the police,

but planned a different route; we all knew
the importance of a good story. Marauding
bands of zealots almost did us in, forced us

to detour around their camps. When I dropped
out at the Temple to buy bagels and a teddy
bear the others went on ahead with the baskets

of gifts; I scrambled to catch up but never saw
them again. No star shone in the darkness;
no sleigh bells jingled in

the air. The evening turned out more bodiless
than I ever dared imagine. By the time
I found the hostel—a rude and drafty barn, shocked

to see the Press already there—the family had
fled, vanished beasts and all without a trace, no
forwarding address. I was disappointed to say

the least; missed connections are the story
of my life. Humiliated too; the shepherds
snickered behind my back. I gave the bagels and

teddy bear to street kids, what else to do?
left that hostile land as ceremoniously as I could,
caught the last caravan to Damascus.

But despite my disappointment a voice
inside my heart kept whispering not to fret,
the family was happy and unharmed. Now

years later, many bizarre and terrible things
have come to pass—too numerous to relate;
but when I think of that freezing barn

I still regret I came too late, never
saw the child, feel a twinge of pity for
the young man who was me, a callow

adventurer in a strange country, benighted and
alone, without a map, no one to thank,
no gifts to unwrap.

Metro Incident

On the crowded Metro subway
a man and woman
            clinging to the T-bar
accidentally rub elbows;
sparks flare out   but I
refuse to look,   pretend
to read my book

            till the smell of burning
fabric strikes my nose and I glance up
in time to see their clothes alight
            like creosote-treated wood,
two Roman candles, acetylene bright.

"Sextaneous combustion," declared the
Globe next day.

The fire chief had sterner things to say:
"Avoid bodily contact wherever possible,"
he warned commuters. "Or pay the penalty."

Despite the grimness of the augury,
the couple made a full recovery.

Sweet Legs

(found poem)

You don't need to put yourself through wax,
hot or cold, to get silk smooth legs.

A combination of camomile, lemon juices,
sugar and water rinses hair from the roots,

but without wax's disadvantages. The mixture
sticks only to hair. That means that you're

more likely to keep that top layer of skin!
Imagine! hair-free for up to 8 weeks between

treatments. And here's the kicker—the natural
combination is water soluble; just wipe any

excess with your reusable cloth strips, put in
a recyclable tin; the result: SWEET LEGS.

Put on SWEET LEGS with your dancing shoes;
the environment will thank you.

Eye-Candy Questionnaire

What are you doing about rough
damaged cuticles and painful hangnails?

Are you building up your body but
tearing down your hair?

Is your small beautiful skin waiting
to be rewarded?

Do you know that a simple anti-wrinkle
cream is not enough?

The air kiss is passé; the hand kiss
is making a comeback and lip-o-suction
is the latest sensation. What are you
doing to perfect your lip-locking
techniques?

Who said that the love of your life
had to be human?

Is Your Life Losing its Edge
(found poem)

Researchers have isolated a unique ingredient that
could intensify your love life—PUNCTURE VINE.

Derived from the Bulgarian vine *tribulus terrestis*
this all natural herbal extract has been used for

hundreds of years. Recently studies show that
men and women who have taken PUNCTURE VINE

have experienced a dramatic surge in libido.
PUNCTURE VINE, TRY IT—IT'S DYNAMITE!

Cosmic Silence

After the ten o'clock news
(another chronicle of doom),
my ulcer flares, I go outside;

stars are peeking from the roof
of night, moon is full,
Hale-Bopp shoots across

my sight, a heart of ice, its
radiance, like ours, borrowed
from the sun. Leaning on

a pillow in a corner of the sky
I spy the Great Huntress;
"Who'll chase away the gloom?"

I say, but she won't reply,
refuses to look me in the eye,
shuts her eyelids tight,

chews her pearly fingernails &
prays.

Queasy Feeling

Woke up this morning
                    a cold-blooded vertebrate
laid out on a
                    white enamel tray,
pale underbelly
                    split open,
slippery entrails
                    —all my mauve inner life—
on vulgar display
                    before the ravening eyes
of the fish-eaters.

Minor Stroke

It's odd, but I don't remember much;
after the nap, I didn't recognize
my black, wool pants; they're not
mine I told Thérèse, denied ownership

of my Florsheim shoes, insisted she
tell me where I was and how I got there;
unable to imagine debility – my vital
signs were fine – I couldn't fathom why

she looked so pale; there was a clarity
in my mind I couldn't find, that's all, and
if she'd just sit and chat with me awhile
the mist would clear and I wouldn't

ask so many questions over and over
until Ruth, my daughter, came and drove
me to the hospital (how unnecessary I
complained). T.I.A.—transient

ischemic attack, pronounced the doctor
next day, his words like polished stones.
You were lucky this time, he said; you'll
have to mend your ways.

Slow Waltz

Don't blame me if I waltz slower,
the hand is reeling round the clock;
we'll all go down to the field together.

There's barely breath to smell the clover
before our little dance is over;
don't blame me if I waltz slower.

When I was younger I cried "faster, faster"
and yearned to whirl instead of walk;
we'll all go down to the field together.

Numbly I watched my first love falter
and blow away like a puff of chalk;
don't blame me if I waltz slower.

Too soon I heard the ploughman shudder,
too late I glimpsed the darkening rock;
we'll all go down to the field together.

Acres of salt ponds I've spilt to recover
the heart's still centre; so don't mock
or blame me if I waltz slower;
we'll all go down to the field together.

Stalker

In the estuary where sky & sea
exchange their silver promises,

he is the cloud on the horizon.
At the Sunday brunch, amidst

sunshine & laughter, he stands
quietly to one side, close

to your shoulder. He is the
unacknowledged guest at

your wedding, the shadow
across your bright hungers

& shining deeds. At night
as you lie under the sheets

of love he coils in the closet
of your heart, only a blood-

beat away. Hush! you can
hear his dark breathing, see

his moon-bright hooves.

Fishing Trip

When my father lay dying I
was in the Laurentians fishing.
Mom phoned, said I'd better
come home if I wanted to see him
                                alive again.
"You're his only son."

Before I'd left I'd driven him
to the hospital—his skin the colour
of egg yolk. The orderly wheeled
him away before I could say goodbye.

The fish were biting—six big trout
in three days.

The evening of mom's call I'd celebrated with
a dinner at Les Trois Biches: Lobster
Newburg, a bottle of Mouton Cadet (white) &
apricot souffle.

I raced home—even picked up a ticket outside
Ottawa—but by the time I reached the hospital
it was too late.

I entered his room, closed the door, sat by
the bedside alone. His cheeks were still
warm & moist.

After, when mom told me they'd made her
sign for an autopsy—the doctors wanted
to see his liver—I smashed my fist
into the wall, stalked up & down the hall
cursing nurses, doctors,

                         accused them all
of indecent haste.

Variations

I

I overhear my old aunt on the phone say:
"I feel badly," & then hang up, hobble back

to the table to tell me Arthur has passed away.
A stroke at eighty-four. Arthur was her

second husband; they were married eleven years,
divorced two years ago.

Then her eyes wander back to the Scrabble
board. "Whose turn is it?" she said.

II

My daughter, who's pregnant with her
first child, drops by for a visit. She's

expecting a millennium-day baby: "I've hired
a duala for emotional support," she says.

"Why not? In this life you only get one turn."

III

Later that evening when we are alone
my aunt slumps in her armchair

in the living room, stares into space for
the longest while. "He came here a month

ago to pick up the last of his things,
you know," she says, "told me he still

loved me." Then she looks at me, tears
in her eyes: "I guess my turn's next."

Lost Child

Seventy winters' snow
unfolded quietly
across the furrow of her days
                                        but no fall of snow can
whiten the greenness of her grief.

She still remembers
the icy farmhouse,
the blue indifference of the sky,
the ragged breathing,
his cold white face cradled in her hands.

Now her skin is infused with light,
the snow, she knows, will soon move in &
his white face will appear again
on the hill between
the white-robed cedars,
call her name

& her snowy voice will answer:
Emmanuel, my Emmanuel.

All Summer Long

(for Palma)

I

Last fall my old aunt was in hospital
dying of cancer, or so we thought;
she won't walk again, the doctor
said, gave her six months to live.

"Doesn't he know our family's hard
to kill," she said, but saw
the notary just in case, made a will,
signed a contract for her burial.

Her only wish, she said, was to swim
her mountain lake, one last time.

II

Now summer's here, she's fooled us all,
totters to the shore on bone-white legs,
slides off the dock into the green dark lake
and pushes out. She has no fear, moves

with natural grace, floats on her back (you
must trust the water to hold you up
she says). All summer long she swims—
each day, one last time—closes her eyes
and lets the sun caress her face, swims
across the bay & back: "I could swim forever."

True Believer

She believed in all the great religions.
She believed in science.
She believed in auras.
In the Big Bang.
She believed in the afterlife.
In heaven (not hell).
The laying on of hands.
She believed in quantum theory.
In progress.
In lunar magic.
She believed in reincarnation.
In horoscopes and quarks.
She believed in Relativity.
In angels.
In flying saucers and ESP.
In dreams she believed.
The collective unconscious and multiple personalities.
In holistic healing.
She believed in out-of-body experiences.
In serendipity.

In brief, she kept an open mind,
believed in almost everything.
Then she died,
crossed to the other side.
Now we don't know what she believes.

The Fire

In the dream he walked across a field
under the palest, silken blue, past

the tall sweet corn, all the way to
the big pond where he dug a trench, circled

it with rocks, gathered bark, wood shavings
twigs, coniferous seed cones, dead

wood, branches for fuel; then, as dusk
descended and fireflies came out he

built a pyre that lit up pond and sky, and
wife, child, mother, father, sister, grand-

parents, relatives, old friends, none dead,
none absent, joined him at the fire,

dark faces polished with love, no one
speaking, as though everyone was seeing

each other for the first time, shriven &
accepted as they'd always dreamed, eyes

picked clean by the long patience of death.

Karen

(in memoriam)

You were only eighteen when you
visited us from Down Under. The

children found your Strine accent
hilarious, remember? How eager

you were! You fell in love
with the cry of loons,

canoeing on Limerick Lake, trying
to glimpse the sly, green bass

banking like planes past the coppery
shoals. How ironic

now to find myself ten years later
watching this video of your wedding,

to see once more the sunshine in your
eyes as you whirl around the dance

floor in your creamy satin gown,
a young bride, caught in music's

arms, the next big adventure
of your life unfolding as in a dream,

blind like us all,
to the dark reef rising

steeply beneath your feet.

In the Cemetery

at St. Bruno de Guigües the residents
are stunned to stone,
the grains of granite graven with earthly loves:
Felix, the forester, has his fondest dream

surrounded by forest, fish & stream;
Pierre, the golfer, makes the perfect swing,
while Yvonne, the housewife, bakes bread
in her oven &
Donat, the carpenter, hits a nail clean.
Only the Curé lifts his eyes up to heaven.

No one cares about the Great Elsewhere.
Heaven is here, the dumb stones sing.

Staying in Control
(found poem)

Pre-planning is easy to put off,
especially if you think

it's going to be difficult or you're
worried you won't get what

you want. But it doesn't have to be
like that. There is a way

to keep it simple, ensure you stay
in control: choose your cemetery

first. By deciding where you want
to be buried as "step one"

your future is assured. Quite simply,
you know where all your decisions

are leading. And you can picture each
step along the way. We're the

Rolling Hills Group of Cemeteries &
we operate five properties

in the Metropolitan area. Beautifully
designed & maintained, each one

is a vital part of the community. And
despite what you've heard there's still

room for you. Yes, it's good to pre-
plan, know exactly

where you're going. Make the only
decision that will last forever.

*I wish to thank once again Susan Musgrave, Barry Callaghan
and Margaret Oldfield for their advice and encouragement.*

*I also wish to thank Tim Hanna and Michael Callaghan and
my daughter Adele Clarke for their work on the design and the cover.*